ALL AROUND THE WORLD
MEXICO

by Jessica Dean

pogo

Ideas for Parents and Teachers

Pogo Books let children practice reading informational text while introducing them to nonfiction features such as headings, labels, sidebars, maps, and diagrams, as well as a table of contents, glossary, and index.

Carefully leveled text with a strong photo match offers early fluent readers the support they need to succeed.

Before Reading

• "Walk" through the book and point out the various nonfiction features. Ask the student what purpose each feature serves.

• Look at the glossary together. Read and discuss the words.

Read the Book

• Have the child read the book independently.

• Invite him or her to list questions that arise from reading.

After Reading

• Discuss the child's questions. Talk about how he or she might find answers to those questions.

• Prompt the child to think more. Ask: Piñatas are smashed at parties in Mexico. What traditions take place at parties where you live?

Pogo Books are published by Jump!
5357 Penn Avenue South
Minneapolis, MN 55419
www.jumplibrary.com

Library of Congress Cataloging-in-Publication Data is available at www.loc.gov or upon request from the publisher.
ISBN: 978-1-62496-919-5 (hardcover)
ISBN: 978-1-62496-920-1 (paperback)
ISBN: 978-1-62496-921-8 (ebook)

Editor: Kristine Spanier
Book Designer: Leah Sanders

Photo Credits: cinoby/iStock, cover; xavierarnau/iStock, 1; Pixfiction/Shutterstock, 3; Czuber/Dreamstime, 4; Florian Augustin/Shutterstock, 5; Matt Jeppson/Shutterstock, 6 (top left); Jamie Robinson/Shutterstock, 6 (top right); Vladimir Melnik/Shutterstock, 6 (bottom left); Patryk Kosmider/Shutterstock, 6 (bottom right); segarza/iStock, 8-9; Danita Delimont/Getty, 10; Jeremy Woodhouse/Holly Wilmeth/Getty, 11; Vincent St. Thomas/Shutterstock, 12-13; Russell Monk/Getty, 14-15; maogg/iStock, 16; Stewart Cohen/Getty, 17; Tono Balaguer/Shutterstock, 18-19; Maciej Czekajewski/Shutterstock, 20-21; Photo Melon/Shutterstock, 23.

Printed in the United States of America at Corporate Graphics in North Mankato, Minnesota.

TABLE OF CONTENTS

CHAPTER 1

WELCOME TO MEXICO!

Explore ancient **ruins**. Experience rich **culture**. Have some tortas. Let's visit Mexico!

torta

Mexico is on the North American **continent**. It is south of the United States. It has beautiful oceans on two sides.

ruins

snake

spider monkey

parrot

jaguar

Deserts and **rain forests** are found here. **Plains** and mountains are, too. The **climate** is warm. It is dry in the desert. The forests are wet and humid. The mountains have cooler temperatures.

Snakes and rabbits live in the desert. In the rain forests, spider monkeys chatter. Parrots perch on branches. Jaguars prowl for food.

Copper **Canyon** is here. It is bigger than the Grand Canyon in Arizona. Much of the area can only be viewed during a long train ride. More than 140 kinds of wildflowers grow here!

WHAT DO YOU THINK?

How do you travel? Would taking a train change what you notice about scenery? Do you think you would see more or less of your surroundings?

Copper Canyon

CHAPTER 2

YESTERDAY AND TODAY

Mayan people lived in Mexico a long time ago. Visitors can still see the **temples** they built. Later, Spanish explorers arrived. They **colonized** Mexico.

The newcomers taught native Mexicans the Spanish language. They shared their traditional music. Now it is known as **mariachi** music. The musicians sing and play instruments.

For a long time, Mexicans lived on farms or in small towns. Now most people live in cities. Mexico City is the nation's **capital**. It is one of the biggest cities in the world.

DID YOU KNOW?

Mexico has 31 states. The Mexican people vote for the president.

Mexico City

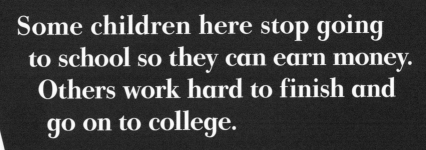

Some children here stop going to school so they can earn money. Others work hard to finish and go on to college.

Many people work in factories. Some farm. Others mine for silver. The most common jobs are **service jobs**. People work as storekeepers, bankers, and teachers.

CHAPTER 3

MEALS AND MORE

The people of Mexico celebrate church holidays, Independence Day, and birthdays. Day of the Dead honors past loved ones. Sugar candy shaped like skulls are part of this celebration.

piñata

Children love to smash **piñatas** at parties. When they break, candy and small toys pour out.

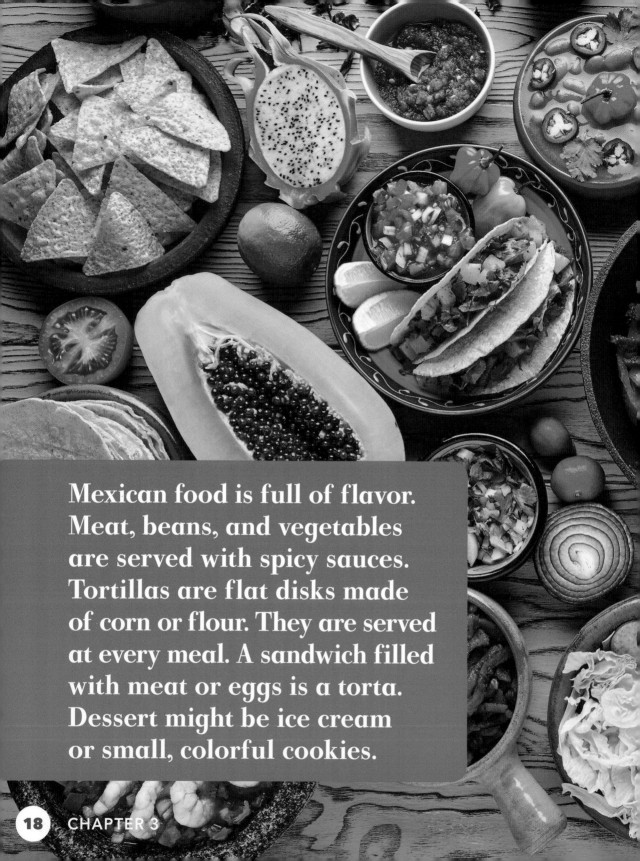

Mexican food is full of flavor. Meat, beans, and vegetables are served with spicy sauces. Tortillas are flat disks made of corn or flour. They are served at every meal. A sandwich filled with meat or eggs is a torta. Dessert might be ice cream or small, colorful cookies.

TAKE A LOOK!

The big meal of the day is lunch. Children eat it after school. Are your meals similar to or different from those here?

 breakfast
sweet bread, hot chocolate

 snack at school
torta, drink

 lunch
soup or salad
main dish (seafood, meat, or poultry)
rice and beans, tortillas and salsa

 dessert
fruit-flavored water

 dinner
bread, soup, or a taco

Artisans are an important part of the culture here. They weave baskets and bags. They make beautiful metal jewelry. Ceramics are painted with bright colors.

There is a lot to see in Mexico. Would you like to visit?

WHAT DO YOU THINK?

Many different kinds of art are found here. What kind of art is created where you live?

QUICK FACTS & TOOLS

MEXICO

Location: North America

Size: 758,449 square miles
(2 million square kilometers)

Population: 124,574,795
(July 2017 estimate)

Capital: Mexico City

Type of Government:
federal presidential republic

Language: Spanish

Exports: manufactured
goods, oil products, silver,
fruits, vegetables

GLOSSARY

artisans: People who are skilled at working with their hands to create a particular craft.

canyon: A deep narrow valley with steep sides and often a river running through it.

capital: A city where government leaders meet.

climate: The weather typical of a certain place over a long period of time.

colonized: To have settled a territory in another country.

continent: One of the seven large landmasses of the earth.

culture: The ideas, customs, traditions, and way of life of a group of people.

mariachi: A type of street music played by a band of trumpeters, violinists, guitarists, and singers.

Mayan: Of a tribe of Indian peoples from southeast Mexico.

piñatas: Decorated, candy-filled containers that are broken with sticks.

plains: Large, flat areas of land.

rain forests: Tropical forests in which a lot of rain falls much of the year.

ruins: The remains of something that has collapsed or been destroyed.

service jobs: Jobs and work that provide services for others, such as hotel, restaurant, and retail positions.

temples: Buildings used for worship.

INDEX

TO LEARN MORE

Learning more is as easy as 1, 2, 3.

1) **Go to www.factsurfer.com**

2) **Enter "Mexico" into the search box.**

3) **Click the "Surf" button to see a list of websites.**

With factsurfer, finding more information is just a click away.